Five White Swans

Other Titles by Lisanne Winslow

Voyaging Pendulum

Sapphires

New Beginnings: A Memorial

Finding Eden Within

West of Boston

In Praise of Creation

Inside the Mind of the Tornado

Inside the Heart of the Tornado

Inside the Soul of the Tornado

A Trinitarian Theology of Nature

A Great and Remarkable Analogy:
The Onto-typology of Jonathan Edwards

Five White Swans

A Poetic Pilgrimage into Ecotheology and Ecospirituality

by
LISANNE WINSLOW

RESOURCE *Publications* · Eugene, Oregon

Resource Publications
An Imprint of Wipf and Stock Publishers
199 W. 8th Ave., Suite 3
Eugene, OR 97401
www.wipfandstock.com

PAPERBACK ISBN: 979-8-3852-2128-8
HARDCOVER ISBN: 979-8-3852-2129-5
EBOOK ISBN: 979-8-3852-2130-1

VERSION NUMBER 07/30/24

Cover Art: Taken from the original pastel painting, "When the Swans Appear" by Luciana Duce-Dugan, MFA, copyright 2021, Prayerful Images, Deerfield beach, FL. *By Permission*.

Author Photo: "Coffee Shop Together" by Sophia Winslow. *By permission*

*to my Mom, Evelyn, for unreservedly giving
the gifts of unwavering faith, wisdom, love, guidance, and
strength to her family and friends*

"*The path goes from the earth into the city, from the soul into the senses, in order to encourage a new experience of God and new human self-experiences in earth's community.*"

    —Jürgen Moltmann
       The Spirit of Hope: Theology for a World in Peril

Contents

Chapter 2: Unfurling the Lifecycle

Chapter 3: The Gospel of Nature and Imagination

Acknowledgments

Any significant work takes a village to midwife into the world. Without my village of colleagues, editors, students, family, and friends, *Five White Swans* would not be incarnated in ink and page. With my heart of love and gratitude, I give thanks first and foremost to my daughters, Arianna and Sophia Winslow for listening to endless lines, giving feedback, and encouragement. You are my inspiration and my joy. I thank my poetry community, *Stone Soup Poetry and Writers Group—MN/CT Chapter*, for their poetic insights and theological contributions to the ecotheology laced throughout the lines. Thank you for your openness and eagerness to hear and reflect on every single poem in this collection over the course of the last several years. A special thanks to Ari Winslow, Halle Ginther, Tim Scheller, and Mike Kluznik for your encouragement and interest in this work. Our bi-monthly Monday night Zoom meetings are a living legacy of my dear friend and founder of *Stone Soup—Boston*, the late Jack Powers, whose commitment to the creative process lives on through our expression of the written and spoken word in all its forms and genres.

I am grateful to my students at the University of Northwestern-St Paul, both in Systematic Theology and in various biology courses. Through discussions in class, in my office, at coffee shops, or at my kitchen table, your creative and spiritual ideas ignited a spirituality of how God speaks messages through a daily encounter with nature. I will never forget the Breakout Chapel prayer walks on the campus island where we met with the *Love that Created* in new ecospiritual dimensions through moss and bird song, in bursting spring buds after a long MN winter, in lake and sky, and through your own sacred writing about God's voice in it all.

I am in deep gratitude for the privilege of spending my sabbatical at Yale Divinity School, engaging colleagues and students in a Trinitarian theology of nature in the classroom and in the forest. I am especially indebted to Dr. Ken Minkema for his warm, collegial welcome at the Jonathan Edwards Center and generously spending time discussing Edwards' philosophy of nature over cups of coffee in his office. Ken, thank you for your consistent support of my work in Edwards' theological use of nature images, always encouraging my scholarship. A special thanks to Dr. Mark Heim, Dr. Ryan Darr, Dr. Mary Evelyn Tucker, Dr. John Grimm, and Mr. Sam King for wonderful discussions on divine action in biology, ecological justice, and the environment over a good meal. Your friendship has enriched my understanding of the impact of ecotheology and ecospirituality in the Christian Church, in all world religions, and throughout the global community.

I thank my congregation at the Mendota Heights Congregational United Church of Christ, MN. Serving as your pastor was one of the greatest privileges of my life. We followed where God led us, out into the gardens and lakeshores, pressing into the very ecosystems where the poet-carpenter of Nazareth himself found communion with the Father of Life. Through Sunday worship, Wednesday night Zoom meditations and studies, and through many creative outings in nature, we lived out the ecotheology and ecospirituality represented in this book. A heartfelt thanks to Lanny Kuester, Megan Reich, Natasha Lee, and Mike Kluznik for their leadership on Wednesday nights, for their dear friendship, and for sharing their own encounters in nature through beautifully expressive and creative ways. A special thanks to Wendy Blomseth for leading us in nature photography as spiritual practice, and for sharing her gift of haiku.

Throughout our lives, there are some friends who transcend categories as colleagues, ministry partners, soul friends, creative partners, caregivers, and spiritual family—*the tribe*. Without you,

I do not know how I would field the storms of life or fully share in its triumphs. To Lanny Kuester, Nancy McCreary, Natasha Lee, Lucy Gibb, Peggy Novak, and Anne McManus, I bow my head and heart in gratitude and love. With patience, commitment, wisdom, and love, you have walked alongside me in this creative project through a very long season of healing. Your walk of faith has enriched and emboldened my own. To Ryan, Holly, Jack, and Summer Anderson, you are our MN family and I am grateful for all of the afternoon walks, collecting specimens, spending time sharing our lives together. To Mr. Dave D'Andrea, thank you for more than forty years of friendship, encouragement, and love. I appreciate your consistent kindness and your strong, unshakable faith.

To my wonderful family, thank you for *all* of the love and support you have given to me over the years in all of my academic and ministry endeavors. I especially thank my mother, to whom this book is dedicated for passing to me her reliance on God and dedication to prayer. To my siblings, Dennis, Chris, and Steven, thank you for your continual love and for putting up with all my pictures of Florida birds and wildlife! We remember Diane and Michael, and our other beloved family members, who cheer us from the other side of this reality and who we think of and miss daily. I thank my nieces and nephews, grand-nieces and grand-nephews for enthusiastically sharing in their crazy aunt's love for the wonder and beauty of plants, animals, stars, and sea with openness and curiosity.

I am indebted to the editors and staff of Wipf and Stock Publishers for working with me on this project, now our second publication together. Thank you for your belief in the value of this work and for your editorial expertise, which has strengthened the book and brought it to its final form.

And, most of all, to the *Love that Created*— thank you, oh Holy One, for creating a stunningly beautiful world filled with images of divine things and spiritual messages for me to spend my life studying.

Introductory Thoughts

As I am writing this, the *Love that Created* gave me my first spectacular sunrise since arriving in Florida to care for my dear mom, Evelyn, to whom this book is dedicated. The expanse of sky out my window right now, how I wish you could see it, is like a broad canvass painted with wide brushstrokes of pipe-like grey cloud-streaks, tipped with hints of pink, orange, lavender, and golden yellow. The praising pre-dawn sky is declaring something that it has declared to towering palms and various plants, to tiny invertebrates teeming, and sometimes enormous vertebrates, for the ~700 million years since plants and animals inhabited a bare earth. Finally, as though the last to the party, the knowing hominin arrived on the scene ~300,000 years ago. The rational vertebrate evolved with the sensibility to feel awe as she looked at the sunrise sky, much like I am this morning, and perhaps at a flitting dragonfly in spring. It was something *phenomenological*, a sense of the sacred, or as Rudolph Otto proposed, "an earliest stirring of the numinous consciousness."[1]

Otto, like others such as anthropologists E.B. Tylor and James Frazer, proposed that for prehistoric *Homo sapiens* the feeling of the numinous, when confronting the powerful and beautiful forces of the biological world, was "a primal element of our psychical nature that needs to be grasped purely in its uniqueness, and cannot itself be explained from anything else."[2] The feeling of the numinous, or sensibility of *the sacred* in the natural world, undergirds our humanity. Perhaps, our species

1. Otto, *The Idea of the Holy*, 122.
2. Otto, *The Idea of the Holy*, 124.

might be better understood, according to James Livingston, as *Homo sapiens religiosus.* He states:

> . . . part of what it means to be human is reflected in our capacity for spiritual self-transcendence. We ought, therefore, to study humans as religions beings, just as widely as we study humans as a biological species, as a political species, or as beings possessed of aesthetic sensibility—if we are to understand human life in its fullness.[3]

The poems in this collection intend to do just that, to unfold a bit more of the understanding of what is to be human, in com-munion with the *Love that Created,* with one another, and with the more than human creatures of moss and bee, terrain and sky. The question for me always is, how does nature move *Homo sapiens religiosus,* and toward what? The poetry in *Five White Swans* seeks to explore this very question. As a companion guide to my two previous theology books, *A Trinitarian Theology of Nature* and *A Great and Remarkable Analogy,* the poems here unfold how the *numinous* that rises in the human heart through our irrevocable connection to the biosphere holds the power to guide us *in. . .* ever-toward the *Love that Created* and to our own interior spirit-selves. It is a pilgrimage toward an ecotheology and ecospirituality that has been with our species and is engrained in our very DNA.

The two previous books mentioned above ground a theol-ogy of nature in a biblically informed metaphysics making the claim that the divine Creator, out of unfailing love, constructed the natural biosphere with an intent to communicate spiritual and divine truths to human creatures who were created to receive such instruction, precisely through the very elements of earth and sky, trees and lakes, cells and molecules. This builds upon the work of the great theologian, Jonathan Edwards, who in the mid-18th century tapped into a dynamic adventure of spiritual revelation through "what has been made."[4] Edwards saw that the

---

3. Livingston, *The Anatomy of the Sacred,* 11.

4. Romans 1:20 " For since the creation of the world God's invisible

whole world is filled with messages from the Divine, "as language is full of words." The poetry in *Five White Swans* translates this vocabulary through distinct spiritual messages whispered by the structures and elements of the everyday world through which we walk and breathe. This genre of ecopoetry is in the spirit of the great nature poets, Gerard Manley Hopkins, William Blake, Mary Oliver, and Jane Kenyon, toward a language of nature, ready to be learned, felt, and experienced.

The first chapter, "Of Organism and Root," explores a relationship with the elements of the natural world that operate in the sense of the numinous toward human mystical experience. In ecopoetics, a vigorous *spirituality* is re-discovered for *Homo sapiens religiosus*; it is an ecological spirituality that speaks to an ancient center within us all that existed before a temple, synagogue, or church was ever built. Here, a much-needed spirituality engages the interior chaotic world of our daily struggle as a gentle communion with the Holy One in the cathedral of sky and sea. These poems seek to capture those sacral moments where emotion and struggle, joy and praise, take on a new vocabulary out of communication from the natural world, directly to the nexus of the human soul. This is biocentrism at its core as conveyed through the lines from the poem, "Visit after Chaos": "In their very biological perfection the/ creatures offer us the solution/ to our chaos." By taking this biocentric medicine, we recover our primal love of nature that holds the promise to heal us, reconnect us, lure us, and inspire us.[5]

In the second chapter, "Unfurling the Lifecycle," the image in my mind is one of a newly sprouted fern fiddlehead young in its lifecycle in early Spring, slowly unfurling to produce the mature fronds of summer. The poems here likewise unfold nature's voice, as the elements of the ecological world again speak

---

qualities—his eternal power and divine nature—have been clearly seen, being understood from what has been made, so that people are without excuse."

5. Biocentrism is a term coined by the theologian, Jürgen Moltmann, which refers to a worldview where humans view the thriving of the earth and all its creatures, in all its sacredness, as central to our way of living for the flourishing of all. See Moltmann *The Spirit of Hope*, 24–25.

to *Homo sapiens religious.* However, this time nature's wisdom teaches vital lessons about the human lifecycle, birthing a new life out of an old life needing repair, or perhaps a life that needs healing and a rebirth from trauma or old wounds. In one instance, it was an apparition of five white swans flying up out of a snow-covered corn field in the Midwest that became a transformative sign. The white swan is a significant symbol in many religious and mystical traditions. For example, in Native American spirituality, the swan represents healing and transformation. In the Celtic tradition, the white swan portrays purity, femininity, and connection with the love of God. Within the ancient Chinese mystic tradition, the swan serves as a profound symbol of spirituality, grace, and the interconnection of beauty between the natural world and humanity. These symbolic elements carry an unburdened message:

> There, the swans became an apparition
> and I opened to their spiritual communication
> offering me a way to reclaim safety,
> waking up to a familiar interior
> that once handled ease of heart,
> *unburdened, do you remember?*

As these lines suggest, nature teaches us that we can heal; it is possible to come back to harmony and balance. Just as nature is a complex structure of interrelationships giving rise to the balance and harmony of ecosystems, so we need meaningful connection to regain our balance, to grow and heal in faith, courage, and love. The poems in this chapter contemplate important relationships and how they change over time, and sometimes they die. In this lifecycle, we become changed in the process. Just as insects must undergo several metamorphoses or "instars," so our lives are a journey of many metamorphoses. We may ask, where is God in these moments? We seek guidance in making decisions, we seek the divine path. In this ecotheology, God speaks to us through nature by unfolding assuring messages to encourage us on the way. In this biocentric ecospirituality, a cottonwood tree gives permission to move on, a pack of raccoons recall courage, a nest leads to security and new beauty. Nature leads. Life does not stay the same. Though the winter may be long, the vernal equinox never fails us, and returns to guide us into our next vibrant season.

In the third chapter, "The Gospel of Nature and Imagination," we find the sacred elements of biology and ecology speaking this time of a life of faith and personal spirituality that can emerge out of an old, worn theology. Systems of religious dogma and doctrine, while still working for some, are for others no longer the inspiring guides they once were. For many, traditional religion has become constricting, damaging, and even toxic. The poems move here in exploratory fashion toward our spiritual birthright as humans, seeking where we might come to discover a living connection with the Divine Source of all life and love. Nature, again as a guide and communicator, reveals some unexpected perceptions. Confession is experienced through a finite heart-shaped cloud. Spring's warm fingers become a caress of God's love, beckoning us not to shy away. In the spiritual practice of solitude, we become partakers of a mystical, sacramental communion with other cave dwelling trogolofauna— "the flat-nosed fruit bat and the Canadian grizzly." Winter becomes a sabbath of contemplation. The earth is an altar. The entire world emerges as a sacrament revealing the presence of a loving, communicative God. Here, it is as if a pair of shears is taken to the religious straight jacket that we may find ourselves in, setting us loose into a spiritual freedom beyond the narrow confines of the ways we *think* God operates. God is officially out of the box. The *Love that Created* is offering an invitation. Those who wish to experience a whole new dimension of knowing the One who *continually* creates, can walk outside and receive. By taking this step, our trek into nature's beauty and mystery becomes a conversation with the One who communicates unceasingly through what has been created, who offers transformation into our fullest and highest expression of *Homo sapiens religiousus*. This exciting, life-enhancing entrance embraces a whole new theology that declares, "here is the real message of redemption: *the infinite cannot be contained.*"

May these poems move you to see nature with different eyes. May you embrace your birthright connection to all that the *Love that Created* is waiting to show you.

—LW

Chapter 1

Of Organism and Root

The Bee and the Orb

The garden is waking up this morning.

The bees in an early
morning meditation
show devotion
to pink nectar-filled orbs.
Their humble determination
sets them to slowly hover and land,
poke about for the treasure they seek,
then amble to repeat on the next.

My prayers amble this morning, too.
In my own humble determination
my mind hovers,
not over a pink nectar-filled orb,
but over the orb of dislocation I am carrying
under breast and skin,
where only the One
who created the orbs
and the bees, the
morning, and me, *sees.*

I poke about for
words and requests that might
adequately present it,
maybe say it just the right way,
and whether I do find
a droplet of nectar or not
the Mystery hears me
and like the bee, I
amble into to the next moment
to search again.

On this bee-tufted morning,
even as out-of-sorts as I feel,
I believe that salutary drops of
insight and wisdom
must be hidden, waiting
with an ancient patience
for me to find them,
again like the bee,
to bring back to the hive
creating sweetness,
sustenance, our home.
And while this contemplation
commences, I am relieved
that harmony still *exists*
in bees and pink orbs and hives
and in *faith*

recalling

what even

the tiniest

drop of nectar

can do,

in nature, and

in this

present

spiritual economy.

Cloud Poem

I woke in a cloud

But it was a beautiful cloud
and I opened my window
to reach out and touch it

Yes, I know how brave that is
because the fog that encompassed
the upper stories of this tall building
was thick, and the rumbling thunder
could be heard, and flashes of lightning seen
in some distant stretch of sky.

Can you touch the storm? I wondered.
Can you feel the cloud?

But as I reached out into its texture, 21 stories up in the sky of the
storm,

there was nothing to feel except the raindrops on my open, wait-
ing hand.

Visit after Chaos

The sea anemones
don't care who won the election.
The long black-spined
sea urchin, nestled in the
crook of a rock, is aware
only of plankton and algae.
The slime fungi on
the decaying leaf in the
rain doesn't take note how
it makes the pavement slick.
The wild geese in V-formation
do not realize the months
of despair they leave behind.
But rather, they all tell us
where peace is found. In their
very biological perfection, the
creatures offer us the solution
to our chaos.
Oh God,
you know where I live.

Chinese Poet, Rescued

"There is the story of the old Chinese poet: at night in his boat he went drinking and dreaming and singing, then drown as he reached for the moon's reflection. Probably, each of us, at some time, has been as desperate."[1]

I came this close to drowning.
It's true.
The splendid, crusty wooden vessel
was painted a faded sailor-blue
with "*Perche Pas*" in
in peeling white letters
on my side facing.
It seemed to be waiting there
maybe thirty years or more
for my arrival.

I climbed in willfully.

Bow-facing, and even
eager to do all the
rowing myself (I usually am),
I pushed off with one
warped and dilapidated oar.

1. Oliver, "*Li Po and the Moon*," 7.

The river that night
was as still as a
monk's mind in meditation.
I thought, then,
of those great bodies of
water that could never
arrive at a mirror-calm,
and my own need, too.

The determined boat gently carved
through the surface
like a sharp knife
through butter,
straightway into the
transparent, knowing dark.

What did it know, the dark and the night?

Well, I was giddy in
delusion, convincing
myself that it was all *just fine*,
being out on this river
at night in this old boat,
even *wondrous*, really—
I was brave, feeling
the intoxicating boldness

of being alive again, when
for a good span the heart
ventricle walls had
solely reverberated
the red ripples of grief.
This was beauty visiting,
and the river, oh so still.

Then the moon came to me,
finally, and so fully.
In a vulnerable happiness
I reached out
over the splintery
wood-worn edge
and tried to swoop the moon
into my arms for a
dance on the water,
when the *splash*
of cold, tea-brown river
hit me in the face,
and I went under.

Like a suction, the
river pulled me down
and I panicked—chastising
my stupid delusion— fighting,
swimming back toward the

border-edge between delusion
and reality.

I could see the real moon's
broad light, up in a far-away
sky, distorted under
the river's flowing lens.

The boat, it had a
cork float bobber painted
red with a white stripe
roped over one side,
trailing behind.
Catching a glimpse I reached
in my desperation, breath held
breaking the water-air skin.
Gasping and gulping, coughing,
frightened, and alone, I held the oval
torpedo-shaped bobber
to my chest, and rested.

I floated on that bobber,
trailing the boat a long while.

I had no idea where
the empty boat
was headed, nor had

any thought of it. I just hugged

the rescuing bobber with

all my life. Floating one cheek

on the surface of the water,

I looked up.

There was the moon, glowing

against the cape of sky,

supremely real.

Dis-Equinox, or Simply Stated— Imbalance

Maybe the geologists
will tell us that the
Earth tilted on its
axis overnight—
and that's why
the leaves suddenly
blushed yellow
and the crimson bee balm
petals unwittingly fell to the ground.

Maybe the acceleration
due to gravity increased
a thousandth of a decimal point
tugging the leaves
off branches, pulling the
thermometer mercury
down, down, down
to this unseasonable frost.

Maybe those natural laws
that have been our only
human consistency

have also turned on us.

What is left to rely on?

The ancient words tell us
to cling to the rock, to run to
the sheets of eternal wings. But
it all feels like clinging to air
and one long, endless running.

And today, when I woke,
the wild geese were honking in tandem.

Contemplation in Snow, Boston

The snow does not fear.
It comes in hurling gusts,
streaming in joyful exuberance
from the heights of the sky.
Inches of banded white
streak tree branches
and railings, coat sidewalks
and cars, roadways
and rooftops.
It falls, lands, and rests.
We shovel, push it into
huge heavy heaps,
clear it away, make room.

Instead, let the drifts
pile where they
may. Observe every
beauty from your
seat at the window,
and when it's time
to go outside,
you will.

The Snow Told the Story, Today

Once, when the snow came,
heavy on the roof of the house,
those blanketed white layers
weighed on me like deposits of gravel,
under strata of nightfall, of the snowfall,
the comfort of an oak tree was
the only company on those nights when the barred owl hooted.

Another time, on a balcony
the snow whispered its tinsel to you,
shiny flecks like sky glitter, and I
might have even called it joy. And once the snow
was so thick that you had to lug
the 6ft Douglass fir
through the patio doors on the deck,
we still have that picture.

It is the same snow, the very same.

But today when the snow came, again,
as it does, it asked this question: *are you truly alone?*
I smiled at the snow from a window

high above the city, and

looked at the ground, swathed

in hope. It was really always there, wasn't it?

Can I Spend Five Minutes Just Watching the Fish Swim?

Thin veils of sweat moisten my forehead. The quiet of the trees gives me a space to reflect on this warm, summer day. I am drawn to the stillness of the great blue heron wading knee-length at the water's edge. At my feet are the remnants of broken, still moist turtle eggs. How seamlessly those little hatchlings emerge into life. Their world knows peace, it is a sacred harmony. Maybe that's why I came here today. Years of endless responsibilities, the constant rush of kids, get her to dance class then run into department meeting… quickly reading agenda notes, students and grading exams, and all of his unfinished business that never seems to leave, the grandfather with mental illness and the family 1500 miles away. Can't I spend five minutes just watching the fish swim? Back in those days it seemed that strength was free, and optimism was given in the offering plate week after week. Today the trees give the offering. Recover. Breathe. Sing the antiphon and let it jump off the page and into the afternoon breeze. The birds said they would carry it for you.

Let Them Come

for Jeremy and Lucretia

I give the
cardinals and rabbits, squirrels,
junkos and finches
ample food at the feeders
so they will *stay*

Their antics and beauty
in proximity to me
make me love them
all the more, and I am
inexpressibly happy

I feel a sacred privilege
by their morning light visits,
as they find nourishment
in my garden. It is
a garden of love.
Is this not
what God
does for us?

Moss Poem #1

"Half a proper gardener's work is done upon his knees"[1]

Brown, loamy stains
smear my pant
leg knees
from digging dreamy
sheets of moss—
thick and luscious
pads of jubilation
I hold in sacred
folded hands,
my most recent act
of prayer.

1. Kipling, "The Glory of the Garden," line 30.

Moss Poem #2

for Dicranum viride and Sphagnum angustifolium

Gentle rolling slopes of

spongy green pillows

hugging water

in a soft, soggy

embrace,

an evolution of

love— moss for water

and water for moss,

both in need of the other—

here, the sun is the

outsider

pulling water and moss

apart. So, they stay together

in shade

protected and joined

in this abundant,

life-preserving

ecology

Ode to Moss

for Polytrichum strictum

The only thing
worthy of writing about today
is getting down
on hands and knees,
a prayer posture
in soft green loamy velvet,
picking off fallen leaves
and insidious buckthorn drupes
in a resolute act of devotion
to the boggy swamp-weed
that saved my life.
Neruda wrote an ode to salt
and a pair of socks.
Maybe he was having a
day (or a life) like
this one, too.

Mend

The morning called me to a prayer-walk
across the forest sanctuary.
Feet touching timberland floor
of stick and leaf crunch, soft moss
happily growing on fallen logs, hands touch
the green cushion and rough bark,
a touchstone that reminds me
do not worry
there is support
everywhere

Observations

The garden is alive
this morning.

Carapaced insects
flit and dart
as microscopic flecks
fall from their unknown source.

It has been a busy night.

Someone has worked,
tirelessly spinning dewy
light-catching threads,
slender veiled tightropes
spanning two wooden rungs
in an interlaced geometry,
a Pascalian artistry
that the wind will
simply blow away.

All the while, the basswood trees
are still busy

pushing forward

millions of their flying

winged seeds, littering

the stone path and wooden deck

in preparation for my

morning spiritual ritual

of sweeping.

Sufficiency

There is no simple
marketing strategy anymore,
the lost are no longer found.

Comfort in mental convalescence
calls out from the blueberries
on the 3rd shelf, the almond butter
and thin crackers, but there is
no nutrition sufficient in this famine.

Somehow the yearling cardinal
has found his way to the
feeder, and the pileated
woodpecker grabs a seed
without permission.

I die a little more each day

and the yellow roses
beg to bloom.

The Red-Winged Blackbird Sits

for Agelaius phoeniceus

The tawny marsh
offers the answer I
can't seem to receive, as
tall reeds and cattails wave
with intention.

They know no other
way of being, no other
place but this one.

Somehow in that
stationary placement, they
breathe content, even with
the dark of winter
soon upon us. These
know no migration.

Slender rods, flimsy
and reckless in the
blowing wind, occupy
this perennial niche.

The red-winged black bird
lands atop a thin, woody stalk
causing a slight bend and sway.

Is it about fit, or a bending of will?

I don't know why
this question has been
with me so long. Yet, somehow
it is so satisfying
not to know the answer.

Even the muddy marsh
in all its pristine wisdom
does not know, as a
bumble bee freely
pauses on the goldenrod.

Namib Desert

In Namibia, there is one of
the driest deserts on Earth,
where the sands glow hot
and the drought is
particularly bad
this year.

A small herd of
stately desert elephants
amble through the sand,
their skin unfolds
like wrinkled drapes drooping down,
their gaunt bodies in migration
to this recalled oasis, and
the young learn the way.
The journey is full of hope,
even with such little green along the way.

But soon they see
that the matriarch
has led her herd
here for nothing.

Precious green pods
meant to nourish,
meant to carpet the
ground in abundance,
are only a thin meagre
trace of the crop that
didn't make it this year.

She looks up and sees
the bursting green branches
just above her reach,
there is only one,
a male, who can reach it
the old female has known him
all her life and has turned
to him for help before.

He reaches the green boughs for her
and for her young
snagging down a branch or two
and instructs, no choice
but to move on. She steps out
into the wide world, again.

Emotional Claustrophobia

Donning the wet suit
plunging the depths
in a nautical archeology
of soul and being.
Sunken treasures were
hidden over decades
beneath the seafloor wreckage.
Sweeping away silt and sludge,
the fine-grained particles
rise in an obstructive cloud.
All I can see
is the black rubber rim
inside the snorkel mask.
In this cloud of sea and sand
I am lost and afraid
in an emotional claustrophobia.

So, sit.
Wait. Live a while in that
confined field of vision
until the ever-flowing
deep sea current,

like the present-moment

breath of spirit,

removes detritus.

Then, all those treasures

will come full

into view.

Interior Parachute Descent

I was thinking of that conversation over tea,
how she spoke of wonder,
a sublime interior *presence*.
Somehow that reminded me
of Machado's poem
and all those wonderful bees
with a golden interior honey
filled with Light.[1]

She said she felt like she was falling from the sky
and *You became her parachute.*

I wondered at the metaphor.

Oftentimes people refer to
falling off the cliff edge
and being caught by a net.
How fearful and fast, the
ruinous chaos of it all, then
an abrupt single-moment
capture with a bump

1. Machado, "Last Night While I Was Sleeping," 87.

and a bungee bounce
undergirded by some sort of free-fall cradle.

But the parachute, now that offers a different image altogether.
Suspended by strings
held in form, hovering above all creation, the far glance
of earth's landscape beneath. A gentle and floating descent,
giving a wider perspective of all that is there,
a bold, expansive vantage.

One might call it, salvation

So, maybe Machado's bees
will come after all,
in more of a parachute descent,
feeling the ground rise to meet your feet.

Stone Walls

Driving the Scottish highlands
is not like driving in Tuscany with
its manic hairpin turns, skeeting wildly between
third and second gear. Scottish
curves are gentle with mercy, the moors
and pasturelands of the shire
slope green all winter long, even as the trees
stale bare, pregnant with blossoms now due.

The Scots build fences to cord off pastures,
wide, broad paddocks in designated benediction
for flocks of grazing mutton, and fields of heather.
Low stone walls frame the plot
like arms in a sacral embrace, holding things in,
not keeping things out.

She drove the shire
through its verdant bends
that praised in oration to an ancient
and receiving sky,
calling to the mystery of the stone walls, all
mossy, masked with
lichen and sea salt.

Here is a theology of rock, round and rough,
where earth meets earth,
picked out from moist peat
soaked in the field of intention and possibility,
where still the crumbles of soil cling to fingers
and wrist and jacket, until the low stone wall
gets built, one stone placed, then patiently another, one by one.
And finally, the light breaking the mist reveals this:
just sheep, at peace, resting in the soft grass.

Voice of Clarification

Swoon wind,
right in one window
and out the other
collecting all those
niffs and particles needing
to be removed.
How they have accumulated,
plugging up vents and pores
with the think-tar
of smallness.
But here, somehow,
lingering stagnancy and dread
are laundered
by a clarifying wind.

They say the sacred voice
is carried on that wind,
how it shades in sweetly,
so gentle and good,
enlivening a stagnant spirituality
like the effect
of the fresh scent of clean air.

I resolve that today I will
fully live.

Where is the Red-Winged Blackbird?

I went to find the

red-winged blackbird

among the cattails and rushes,

but when I arrived

I found that they

already migrated.

How lonely

the lakeshore is

without them.

Centered Opening

The earth is
becoming green, again.
Faces on the
streets smile at life birthing,
above them, around—
green spray
dispersing the brown,
worn-out gray dinge.

There were
branches once,
that spoke of death to life,
the resurrection
that is always
at the end of the equation.
Today, the equation
is still being solved,
so many variables.
Regardless, spring comes.

Fingerlings of green
push their way up through soil

ardent with persistence,

and the forsythia

faithfully flame yellow.

Can one say that spring lies?

Never.

It always speaks

this truth to the wakening

creatures of the earth: *you are not extinct.*

You are here

incarnating another spring,

and perhaps even

another summer,

another fall,

another winter—

   you are here, there is life.

Look out your

window, the

trees are preaching.

Of Soil and Dough

Cupped hands, down on knees,
postured with
watering can and gardening gloves
scooping soil the way my grandmother
with bare hands scooped flour from the bin
and with a few drops of water she
made dough for little fingers
to plump and press into shapes
that could only be recognizable
to a 4-year-old's mind,
a dog, a flower,
oh, she could see them, too
it was her simple act of love
in flour and water in dough
at the old wooden butcher-block table.
For today, soil and water
form another kind of dough
and another kind of loving
but the question is the same to me somehow—
Oh, what beautiful thing just happened?

The Lesson of the Spider

This crumply busy spider
suspends from a trampoline
of self-made slender threads.
Teeny, gnarly, curled legs
pinch and crawl,
as if each its own knitting needle

The breeze comes,
the trampoline rocks and
quivers vibrato.
In immediate response, the
arachnid folds into itself armadillo-fashion
until stillness is returned

The shadowing clouds part
as a silver shine-beam knifes down
from the sky, reflecting each slender lineage
that connects pole to fence to overhead awning—
a structure that took many
of the nighttime hours to construct, *de novo*

She lives on this swaying trampoline of fragility, for today.

An afternoon shower deluge and—swoosh— it's washed away,
she's tossed into a bush!
But don't worry oh sweet reader,
she will build again

New silk-like blessings will flow,
streaming from her
underbelly spinnerets, *at will*
as she again finds herself
on the threshold
of this free,
eternal moment

There is Always Light

Even in this stygian smog
reeking of discouragement and humiliation
a phosphorescent emission
of courage presents itself
within, if only surfacing as a momentary
flash—*it is there*
and in the crepuscular dim
of the illusion I hold dear,
you know, the one in whose purpled, secure darkness
I refuse to release,
there is a truth that quietly wakes behind
like the angled trail
of the long-time cone of light
fading along the skin of the early morning pond

It is trying to convince me one more time.

I pray it is not scorpions for breakfast, again.
Then I hear a faint sound,
the morning dove's
paean hymn of deliverance
has arrived

Winning the Battle on Terror

The troubled soul.

His, a microcosm of
chaos, fear, violence,
and he says, even terror—
thunder is his teacher and
fire is the mortar,
burning to resorb the healing
contained within the
closed system of his body.

They both know

All of the world's calm beauty
bids healing and safety,
come into the ground of outright abundance,
wherein the internal fear-microcosm
might experience presence.
The murderous unfriended abyss
will be soaked in the spray
of the fountain of all goodness,
saturated in the shower of light.

Hers, an ecosystem of
being relying on being, interdependence
of species on species
in the food web of loving.
And in the complexity
of organism and root,
sand and clay,
creation depends on the foundational
trophic level, the
primary producers incorporating the light of love.

But it is not as though she has *never heard all of this before*:
    interior darkness,
    inland heart chaos, fear,
    terror, violence,
    don't-want-to-hurt-you

Always, and at all times,
calling forth light
from the bitterness
of nothing.
The revelation waits
for receptive clay.
Sometimes, the microcosm
convulses beneath the weight,
unsure of another world.

Therein lies this
one reverberating theme,
as common as the
changing climate
within her ecosystem—
he walks away, his fear
wins the day.

Retreating, the light of love's
compassion and goodness
rejected
choosing rather to comfort the
chaotic fear,
to nurse it,
to live inside of it.
In the quiet of her own tears,
she has seen
the result.

At day's end she closes
her eyes softly,
whispers the one recurring warning
not to slip away good lives
as hostages to fear,
and she prays.
Shalom

Chapter 2

Unfurling the Lifecycle

Five White Swans

for Cygnus columbianus

The burden of grief has an inevitable departure.
The message came on the wings of the returning
tundra swans that day. Five of them,
one lost a life mate.

Somewhat surprised, I found
relief there, shedding Nietzsche's *agon*
for the settled assurance that
there is no end to the quest for the illusive "real answer"
only finally recovering
the clear pool of peace within, instead.

The five white swans, as they flew
in mysterious union
above the snow-covered cornfield,
showed just how to crack the illusion
of that version of truth,
which doled out a raggedy burden of future,
one that I nervously held for decades,
maybe even, generations.

There, the swans became an apparition
and I opened to their spiritual communication
offering me a way to reclaim safety,
waking up to a familiar interior
that once handled ease of heart,
unburdened, do you remember?

This time, I will fly alongside the white swans,
realizing that the illusion distorted my vision at first,
it was like a windswept updrift of snow into a white sky—
but look closely now, it is not snow at all
it is the arrival of the tundra swans
flying upward and free
into that wide open horizon yet to be seen.

This time, I will move
beyond a mere acceptance of that worn power,
into the spiritual union
that has beckoned me
to fly, at last

Canticle

"Could the world be about to turn?"[1]

There is no use clamoring over regret.

The reverse crystal ball

can never serve

to change what was,

unable to remove the ingredients

you tended with such careful

contemplation to

produce the

taste of now.

And really, would you want to?

Who knows what *that* flavor

might have been?

There is only one truth:

      The path led to here

The sooner you accept

that all other paths

were mere speculation

with fantastical outcomes,

1. Daigle et al., "Canticle of the Turing," line 6.

the clearer the soul will be

to take the next

necessary step.

Look at the list, again.

Didn't every next step *feel right*?

Every opening, *an offering of promise*?

The world is about to turn

and into the meadow of

uncertainty you have taken a step.

There, you have discovered the secret.

Only the next right

decision exists. Just

as it always has.

Awareness

Where is my terror?
Where is my peace?
The train whistle blows
through the chill and dark
of the pre-crepuscular silence
and the ache is right there
it stings like salt
until the memory
of soaking in the warm
cherry blossom-scented water
of the bathhouse in Misaki
wakes me up.
I have been asleep
in my life, again

The Next Instar[1]

I used to rule the world.
Now, I dance a swayed dervish
with outstretched arms
caching the warm rain at sunset

I used to order the disorder,
felt the calling to straighten up
all the unruly messes.
Now, the blooming roses grow
wild on vines unashamed

I used to call myself
the one needed.
Now, the need is *mine*

The tight rope is still strung taut
between high-rises forty-five flights in the air,
but on that one day
I was the one who jumped off
and my body took flight
into the fidelity of freedom

---

1. Instar here refers to the molt between metamorphoses in terrestrial arthropods/insects.

And the farther I see

the tall prairie grass

waving in the rearview mirror

the closer I am

to the sanctuary of soul

Thinly Veiled Words that Float in My Memory

There is
so much
brokenness.
So, we make
fragrant tea
and talk.
Not that
it will solve
anything,
it never really
does. But it
makes us
feel as if
it does.
Words fly
on air
and race
around, sometimes
they settle
down like
dust, only
to be wiped

away with a

clean, white cloth.

That was

yesterday,

the day when

you were here,

and words

could be

exercised in calisthenics.

Words now

come from

only one side,

floating in all those images.

Memories help.

They whisper—

all that was lost,

will be found

Being Carried Far Down

Again, in the still

of suspension

with that old sac flung over

my shoulder

being carried

so far down

into the absence

of wonder

where the lone barred owl

calls out to me through ancient trees

with no one to interpret

except the soul—

and the soul knows

in its terrestrial intuition

of that other place

inside presence

where no absence

exists,

only the giving

and receiving

of gifts

Cottonwood

Maybe the cottonwood trees
will float their fleecy tufts
without my witness
next year.
No eyes holding in gentle gaze
that day of beginnings
when feathery windswept seed
floated in a constellation
over a different river
than this one. It was
a life of collecting gems
at twilight.

Couldn't learn
to love it here. Couldn't
seem to make the memories my own.
The memories seemed
too small, wishing they were
attached to someone
else's life, perhaps
someone who cared
to mourn them properly,
and miss them.

No paddle boat cruise,

no cottonwood. No future,

despite what the ring said.

A life worth wanting

calls to me from my future self,

I find myself listening, as wind blows

through different trees

Delusion

Maybe this
is freedom—

letting go
of *that* delusion.

There is warmth
by the fire.

Exploration

for Ari

Isaiah 42:8–9 "See, the former things have taken place, and new things, I declare, before they spring into being"

Just walk out your door.
There, you have just taken
the first courageous step.

The lighted tree-lined street
walks you out of your own dimmed interior.
Then you can decide if you have
found life there, or not. Oh, I don't mean the illusion

of those thousands of busy people walking
like living zombies toward the stoplight corners. Rather, this:
check within you today, what are you carrying there? What
exhilaration begins to show up, or not?

Maybe dribs and drabs,
alive, asleep, fantasies of that one day still not coming,
a watery soup of uncertainty cooking in the pot of
all that unknowing, yet it is still yours.

Be in wonder

with how you breathe life,

how this moment of

pioneering belongs only to you,

see what you will do with it,

and what will come to you

in unexpected reward

for just this stepping out. It is

a re-acquaintance. The bustle of

discovery— what's out there,

but maybe, what's been inside. You

will find, it has all

been waiting for you.

She Who Brings Me Delight

for Ari

Her heart is a tray
of carefully prepared dates,
sticky with honey, stuffed
with savory cheese. She is a
meal prepared for a table-full
of people eating and laughing, olive
oil in a bowl for dipping bread.
Sometimes she is a single fish
caught in a net, and other times
as Jesus says, 'Cast the net on
the other side"— *and she does*
and it fills in abundance, deep red
like pomegranate seeds in a bowl.
Getting lost around the twelve gates
of Jerusalem, she finds the one door
that leads home. She is the lone flower
blooming in desert sand, she is the rain
that causes dormant seeds to grow,
her light shines, courage was here all along

She Who Makes Me Smile

for Sophie

She is the laughter that floats
in moments of the ridiculous
reminding me just how easy
life really is, she is the glistening
spontaneity of fun when we
at a moment's notice
jump in the car and go—
her comfort is the simplicity of siting
on the couch in silence, yet together,
her smile fills the gaps where life has
sapped out the green and the flowing stream.
She is the lily clothed in greater
splendor than Solomon, she is the
green vine flourishing in the creativity
of a complex molecule drawn to perfection.
She is the star in the constellation of love
unafraid of the night because
it is there that her light gives
light to the world

Gravitational Constant

for Sophie

Psalm 103:11 "For as high as the heavens are above the earth, so great is God's love"

In the sky of wonder for
how it all works, the drive
for knowledge of mechanisms
stirs your curious soul. But it
is more than just
the chemistry of lab and molecule
it is the connection of soul and matter,
the calling of depth
to a life reaching
its hand to you,
one dreamed and grasped.
The biotic and astral mysteries
are offering themselves to
your finding,
pluck them and take them
as your own, given to you
from the celestial heights
of the greatest love,
you were called
to this empowered, sacred moment.

He Held the Glass for Me

Early morning, quiet meditation. Crows caw overhead in the little
Japanese house. In another setting their screeches would be eerie.
Nothing can be eerie here. Tatami mats, rice paper doors showing
the dance of early morning shadows of bamboo canes. The little
girls are asleep on the floor in the next room. He, the one who
held the glass for me, the one whose lips softly kissed the base
of my neck, is half a world away. But today, the little Japanese
house holds me, holds this silence; holds us, a mom and two little
wild-haired girls. I remember the night when I walked to the lab,
and the girls stayed behind in the cozy warm house. They were
old enough, they said. They weren't afraid. But then, the wonder-
ful story of how they fought off the raccoons, who came to feast
on the pile of acorns they collected earlier with Kaikuro, the little
spikey-haired boy who lived next door. They heard some commo-
tion out back. They looked out the door. Raccoons. Lots of them.
Oh, the peels, the exhilaration, the terror of it all… "Mom! There
were raccoons!! A pack of them!! We yelled through a crack in
the door!" Triumph. Then, when courage was free.

Contentedness

Stone arched balcony,
someone lives there,
maybe wishing they
could move back
home to that warm, green
country without all this
god-awful snow—
as the girl across
the street looks out
her window and wishes
she lived there

I Compute the Weight of the Letter L

It asks so much of us,
that letter—
pulling extremities out from
heart's depths
where the effects
of affection leak out
ad extra
despite all efforts
toward self-protection.

Don't want to repeat *that* herstory

But I again compute
the weight of the letter L,
the risk-benefit analysis
love and loss
yet again, I muse—

> *can't do this again*
>
> *must do this again*

perhaps the sky-scraping deciduous trees
ponder this, too?

Buds parallel their naked twigs,

the leaf out, the long lilt of languid summer,

leaf litter,

loss, lonely winter—

Oh, the weight of that hideously lovely letter

holding in its monarchs' scepter

the power to wield the decree:

heart's longing fulfilled, or the pain of loss.

And we know that love is always both

In the Wild Nest

"But his own nest, wild nest, no prison."[1]

There are iron bars
around this city,
this state, even—
invisible though they are
to some. What once
offered freedom and beauty,
the only future dreamed into
being, with years of prayer

has now morphed into a
translucent prison, where the
moon's slivered light
has made off with adjacent possibility,
leaving in its trail
the likelihood
of nothing.

One wonders if the
wild nest exists anymore,
or, more profoundly,

1. Hopkins "The Caged Skylark," line 11.

if it ever did? Was the vitality
of delight in the wild nest,
the one that was her own nest,
only an illusion
after all this?

If so, perhaps
that's not so bad.
Even illusion itself
enters the room
like the sky

Laugh, A Lot

The blob of jam that fell
off the spoon and onto the floor
was actually a moment in the ridiculous,

missed the crisp toast altogether
and leapt acrobatic through the morning air
hitting the floor with a gentle, but elegant, plop.

And then there were the hurried words that came out in a back-
flip,
the keys that eluded your notice
until sitting behind the wheel, the two
unmatched socks that made it on your feet,
the wrong turn taken as the mind created its endless lists.

Laugh, a lot. Why not?

Ridiculous episodes
float in like visitors, bringing into the
flurry of the day a moment to pause,
to notice the uncontrollable, unpredictable
nature of moment-by-moment living.

If only the jam stayed on the spoon as it should

If only the socks behaved themselves in the drawer and stayed paired

If only life would simply obey all of our rules—

But life, the unpredictable rogue that it is,

will not always obey the rules,

even, and precisely, when you feel it should.

No, every light will turn red the day you are late,

the milk jug will run empty,

the phone call will surely be missed.

Perhaps, resist the inclination

toward the smallness of frustration.

The wild forest, messy and unpredictable,

gives you its ancient wisdom: the snow will

arrive too early and melt too late; the blight

will wipe out leaf and tree, the heat will

scorch and burn.

All of this misbehaving

is happening

under biological laws *we fully do not know*

yet in the mysterious ecology of harmony

balance is miraculously maintained,

the seeds germinate, the soil

is soaked and nourished, everything grows.

Let all your frustrated worry-energy
move like a winding river
toward a different destination. Smile
in your most ridiculous moment,
laugh along with the
wild rogue who sent it
to help you let go of all that blind control.

Throw up your arms at last,
and be blessed in the gentle knowing
that you, within the ecological
order of things,
are alive.

Angiosperm Regeneration

i.

When I flourished,
when the mysterious
glory-streamed wonder
captured the blooming
garden of awakening
within me,
I was like the wild prairie,
reaching with childlike arms God-ward.
Yet, in that midsummer beauty,
when intellect and creativity
accelerated at cheetah-speed across the
savannah of mind,
I was producing, as all flowers do,
the next-generation seeds.

Could I have known it?

No. I thought the blaze of
abundant curiosity,
the high summer of science-imagination-soul-movement
was my being-in-God, the

who-I-am-in-myself
living in the happy state
that perennials feel
in late summer
after sufficient, soil-nourishing rain.

But I see now

I do, I see this botanical cycle of blossoms
in their color-soaked
pageantry of success, existing
not for that single summer
but to produce seeds—
to multiply their very selves.

But to do so they must die back,
let their former beauty
wither into autumn brown,
seeds fall, *disperse*,
some are blown far away
like dreams hovering over the vast sea.

The despair arrives, *it must*.

The vaporous darkness stalks, the
fingernails of the wind scorch
every frozen thing in an isolating chill,

yet these are the necessary conditions
for the dormant seeds enfolded in
the kind embrace of the rich soil bed,

> *when ice crystals reorient molecules*
> *when time stops for a while*
> *when they think they are dead*
> *when they lose faith*

when they believe they will be dormant
and useless forever, in the
ice-encased potential
residing beneath the thick seed coat.

It had to happen,
you know what I mean.
It was biking along the Charles River,
hiking rainforest paths,
studying the edge of the sea with students;
all these meadow flowers
of the soul,
they all required the botany of
the timeless dark faith
yet again to deliver, a brilliant, color-sprayed
garden of light.

ii.

I bloomed where I was planted,

flourished and produced seed,

so many seeds

in *students*

> *lectures*

> *knowledge dispersed*

> *research, publications,*

> *sermons, prayers*

the plant grew and grew and grew.

But the pot grew too small,

far too small,

and the plant body drooped in exhaustion

leaves withered and choked

lacking nitrogen and even water

> *to survive, to thrive*

> *to transform and grow*

a larger pot was needed

or even a backyard spot

in the garden, in full sun.

iii

Transplantation is

traumatic to the plant.

I remember the day

I purchased the divided
bee balm perennials
from a lady selling plants on the cheap
out of her backyard,
bare roots washed free
from the protective sticky soil
plunked into buckets of water
it was jarring to see it
vulnerable, unprotected,
out of their necessary environment
of loam and microbe,
roots stood naked, undernourished
stripped to the barest essential,
my only inclination was
to get them back into the womb of the earth
into the love-ecology of safe soil
held secure, nourished, well-*being*.

iv.

Here, the sun never stops shining.
The grass never stops receiving
the morning dew,
the Saw Palmetto and Gumbo Limbo
never have to contend with frost.
The great blue heron
statuesque and still
wades knee-deep in

tranquil thought,

contemplating life's mystery

found in the simplicity

of the next fish caught.

A readied consistency exists

in the quiet act of paying attention.

Just this once let me seek

the erudite peace,

the germinating efflorescence,

the boundless micro-climate

of right resolve

What to Think About in an Afternoon in Autumn

I can't
think about you
right now,
the long slender
red pine needles
are mysteriously turning brown
while the rogue squirrels
and I are in a battle
over my tulip bulbs.
Priorities, you know.
So, I will have to think about
you later, or
tomorrow, or never—
you, oh memory
of myself,
cherishing Chagall's
poetry in French,
sifting black
grains of Icelandic
sand, taking it
home in a jar.
There is no

day, there is no evening,

there is no night,

only now

as the Chinese

silver grass turns

autumn red

Over the Garden Wall

The trace of mist in the
unassuming poise of morning
reminds me
as I can see my own breath
on the exhale.

The long bygone burdens stagnate
tight-lipped in the past,
yet their lessons
are here, *right here.*

The white Icelandic
sweater still has hints
of the back of the closet,
the haybale snoozes there on the porch,
the basket of grotesquely bumpy
orange and green gourds audaciously
pluck up courage,
the corn stalks keep falling over
and, of course,
the pumpkins
remind us all
of why we are here

The Crime of Longing

Leaning back
on the cold, damp wall,
hewn and rough,
exhaling in a thin vapor,
I take a moment
here, to think.

Perhaps the
crime of longing
was not in
desiring the freedom
from captive grief,
nor in calling
out in despair's womb
for the miraculous
birth of wonder,
but was in the
avoidance of reality's
loud screaming,
as if I could
outrun reality, as if
it would never catch up.

But how

could I know

that we were

running through

puddles unseen? There was

no way to turn around.

Reality caught up

and the crime of longing was solved.

Time to hear

what reality was shouting

back there all the while:

pause, see that which *is*.

How will you ever know

what visions were passed

along the way?

Two Years Since

He wiped away the
blackened smears
of the lines
she so carefully
painted before.
Heart, still in the
ache, the refuge
place where
no prayers rise
anymore

It was a tender act

Yet receiving doesn't
come so easy. And, for
two years now,
this cloak felt
heavy,
especially today

They noticed
bread still sitting

on the table, and the little pill
that offered life.
How odd
that an inert
purple tablet
held out hope

But the real
generosity
was that hope
arrived,
from dandelions
sprouting in pavement
from the note found under the floorboards,
out of the smile of yellow paint,
through cool streams in air vents and cracks in
the glass.

Somehow it doesn't matter,
you know
you'll take it
from anywhere.

As the Sun Ascends in Confident Resolve

In the early
matin of prayer
I rise
one eye open
with this same question
dragging me into the
confessional of the morning

Drawing scenarios in
my mind
as an offering,
hoping you will
pick one of these,
and answer

Thoughts and emotions
vine through my mind,
imagining an existence

     a resurrection

of sorts where even the
mourning sisters of Lazarus rejoice.

But the answers keep
coming in as *no*

Is the *no* already
inside of me? Contemplation
guides the inquiry and
I am given this insight:

> *Stalled resolve somehow feels better*
> *than making the fearful decision*

Perhaps the gymnastics of
waiting, with all the interior
turmoil and seeking and praying,
and pleading—
has been weakness, rather than faith.
The fearful need for certainty,
is not faith, at all

Attending orange beams
appear on the wall opposite my window,
warm light
competes for every available space.
The sun ascends in
confident resolve, this too
speaks of faith.

Rooftop with My Sister

for Diane

In the evening,
the speckled smear
of the Milky Way
peeled across the
cape of sky
as if on tip toes—
we climbed out the
window of your bedroom
onto the flat rooftop,
silent so mom wouldn't hear

We entered that liminal space
as though the night
quietly invited us
into the commonwealth
of joy

Immortal

The scroll
that tells their story
still hangs
on the wall
all green-matted
with inked sable-hair
brushstrokes
that carry pain like
flying swans across
the rice paper page

He recalled the
cold winter afternoon when
they shared a bowl
of small red
potatoes with butter
and salt. He said
he liked it that day
in the driveway of
their shared humanity
when she traced
the rough tar

of his cheek

in a borrowed streak

of tenderness

She recalled eating one potato

with a fork, and

leaving him

the rest

Poem of Commencement

This was the beginning
of who I was to become,
a September of the
academic year that lasted twenty,
commencing students in classrooms
watching furious pens
move over the exam page,
a knowledge of yearning
for *their* knowledge,
I was an instrument, the pen
that wrote the love letter to nature
on their hearts,
the dissection tool
that cut into their delusion of
expecting the easy way,
reflecting the underlying tissue
of grueling study
with blood and tendon
producing *that scientist* who
walked across the stage
on diploma day

I became the high ideal to live up to
I became the quest for revelation itself:
the one great idea that sets apart the many.
I became the dream of the heights
they could reach, of course

I gave that to them.
And, to me.

On this day, the final day,
the campus green
reposes in silence
waiting for my good-bye.
It will not soon forget, nor will I,
as I ponder the grassy slopes
and cascading fountain
as if already in my memory

We have grown, we have cried,
the *yet to become* has begun unfurling
like tender fiddleheads in summer,
flying geese overhead follow a far-off call,
the sun is reduced
into the open hands of prayer,
the final commencement

The Middle Way

A single goose
flies overhead
calling out it's
throaty honks—
driven toward
the direction of
the doppler response
calling her home

Chapter 3

The Gospel of Nature
and Imagination

Imaginative Prayer

"To ask anything of God but God alone is to invite spiritual bankruptcy"[1]

Abide, he said.

Poems, pray with them

or music, pray with it,

in joy or sadness

lean into the offenses of the heart.

Recover nature, wherever you are,

like on the day when you prayed in the

cathedral not made with hands.

Summon images that urged you,

pray the gospel of imagination.

Be bold as you bewitch faith

into becoming what it has never been.

Permit the paint pallet to become your sacrament, the

poem on the page the icon of deliverance.

Watch the walls of dogma crumble, then

use the crumbs to create a collage of courage.

Open the box and let God out,

meet the God above God who lives

so lovingly in your

1. Rumi, *Rumi Day by Day*, 149.

imaginative freedom.
Know the unashamed life
in this arrival, and Presence
will finally consent to
what glory really means

Ancient Words

I don't know what to do with the ancient words today.

faith says believe

mind says let go of delusion

heart says, resurrect hope

being says, you know where to find peace

They are all correct.

Then, after the long contemplation of such things,
one wonders if healing
is actually possible,

or if the heart passage
is only an exercise

of incurring wound
upon wound

until you finally
come to your senses,

and stop

Remember the Word Intention

It has all been here, patiently
waiting for you.
Look beyond the window's dreary landscape
into the garden of soul
to see it is all still there

Once, despair had its way with you
and you thought it was all over,
saying you would never have any of it again

But you did the right thing,
you let despair wreak it's havoc until
the day when you could finally give
yourself love and compassion

An unrestricted entrance opened
healing the gummed residue of grief,
and you found the deep roots
of remembered ways
of living

As you listened, the inner wisdom whispered these intentions:

peace of mind and peace of soul
this confidence
stability
affirming connections
wisdom and guidance
free inner bondage, release

The intentions remind you
to *trust the process*
as you rummage
for the bright spot
that made the world a good place
before the wreckage.
It happened. You have survived it. *Now think of that.*
Goodness has made it so.
But you still ask, why then the wreckage?

Now you have arrived at the right question

There are many lesser
answers embedded in the one great answer,
which is this: *you are not meant to be small in this world*
It is not your pain
that makes you small, but the despair

Its muscle crushed you under.
But your true source,
the intent of the heart,

is the dominion
where despair can never live, for long

Come now, into the spacious place you own,
the fragrant, flowered summit
where not one wondrous
sequence of light has left,
where all those intentions
have patiently been with you

in anticipation of meeting,
waiting only for you to be ready

Arrive, and remember who you are

Being in Essence

~Inspired by Rev.Dr. Emil Brunner (1889–1966)[1]

Embraced by Being-in-essence is like entering
cool streams that call the body
into the whisper of water,
enveloped entirely in a languid pool of liquid love,
a fluid dream where you could simply float away

Yet, in this air-like bouyancy
there is an ever-enduring Ground, sturdy
as the earth's mantle beneath our feet, holding us up now,
without ever even having to wonder whether it will, *or will not,*
it just does, it simply is

This abiding love-as-strength,
faithful, gracious, oh so gentle
and ever pouring forth in Self-giving
as God is in God's Self,
the reason why there is something,
rather than nothing

1. Brunner, *Revelation and Reason*, 45–47.

And yet, this loving *into* us, is at the same time
a persistent *will* to communicate that we
are radiantly loved

And I am reminded
of that saturating morning
when the sunrise, a photonic rhapsody,
flooded into and through my window
carrying a message: *I am here...*
there was sight in the eyes, thin delicate membranes of retina,
rhodopsin, and nothing could deny it: *As God is.*

The divine degree of
creation is the content of Self-revelation.

If the hyphae connecting
every tree, the pigment in the
hummingbird's iridescent feather, the atom and molecule,
gene regulation, and enzyme-substrate perfection
—*all that was created*—
communicates messages of the beauty
and enduring love of the Being-in-essence
how then shall we love and protect this world?

Answer

You hope for a visitation
You wait for the wisdom to come
You beg for forgiveness and healing
You believe in the light to heal

You trust in the ancient promises
You act in obedience and love
But you forget the words the poet-carpenter taught us
They will also do it to you

It becomes the perpetual winter with no Christmas
Being betrayed for a piece of Turkish Delight
A crucifixion with no resurrection
The long dark night never dawning.
My God, I did not see it,
This is the answer.

Cycle of Inevitability

The desert mothers
knew this.
Get yourself
out of this cycle.
Night in the desert
gives way
to the light of day
which brings hope
and relief, only to
give way to the
darkening night,

then the true dark

and so it goes.
You need to find
your freedom.
That way into
the world of
palpable living
released from
the cycle's inevitability,

the freshness

and wonder

of an ancient love

never leaving

that provides luminosity

as brilliant as the colors

of the Aegean. That old

ugliness wanes and dissolves;

what's left: the germination

of beauty

Here, the Moment of Healing

The moment
when you realize
that you had it all along,
is when you can
be assured
that your healing has arrived

Wise Matrons

They saw
the world reeling.

As receptive oracles,
they predicted.

So, in wisdom
they renounced
the way of the
inevitable,

choosing to
disembark the
wild ride of pain's absolutism
all that brokenness with no justice,

for the anchor-hold
of their own construction.

There they found beauty.

The feeding birds pecking at seed, the cup

of tea with sugar,

honest work and honest prayer.

Just this simple recipe:

Complication breeds discontent

New Morning Prayer

Now I know
why the monk
left his begging bowl for the mountain,
and why the desert mothers and fathers
left for the caves—
the world becomes
no longer safe,
commitment is exchanged for selfishness
kindness for cruelty,
faithfulness for lies,
love for detachment.
The only peace now
is the offering of snow
gently falling out my window

Poem Musings for To-day

What would I do
if I had a hundred
hours to sit under the
fig tree to think
and read and meditate?

Would freedom
lift up the sagging heaviness?

Would I dream of home, family, security, future,
love, hope?

Might solitary peacefulness be
somehow given for figs
in exchange?

Advent

When life was large
we all sang Silent Night
as the candle glow flickered
on the old damp stone walls of St. Macher's
and the wind hummed in medieval harmony
with the pipe organ's tall lungs.
All the while, outside, the wild North Sea
sang yet another hymn

And since then, life has
grown small—

There is the lush green
yard-grown moss,
a baby foxglove that appeared
on the garden floor,
the morning sun's
vocabulary is translated
through filtering tree branches
in a shining crucifix of light,

miracle

Resolutions

Release the continued tendency
of incessant activity
in exchange for pause

Allow all the thinking
to dissolve into the
sunlight smoothing
swiftly over mounds of snow
that drift above the softening cadence
of the distant hills

Let the soul rest
from all the years
of arduous prayers
where supplication melts, finally,
into the simplicity of silence

Receive grace, *no effort*.
Exhale that cloud.
It has been raining inside of you
for far too long.
Then, can you see how all those questions

just lose their power?

Freedom breaks open

a hole in the sky and nothing else

seems to matter except

this receptive

form of prayer

Disturbance

The mystic said,
"Let nothing disturb you"
but in her calm and
peaceful cell
penning these lustrous words
by quill and candlelight,
could she have ever
known *this*?

        betrayal, lies, abuse, abandonment, injustice
How to manage
the interior castle
when the castle was besieged
by the very ones to whom
trust was given?

Prayers come forth
before dawn,
the rational mind
denies them.
Faith becomes the battleground
and when the call came in
that the battle was over

everyone lost.

And He asked,

"will I find

faith on the earth?"

Vestigial Faith

"Bring us back," they asked,
after the long,
dark winter,
after a promise was given,
holding the goodness
they knew to be true,
not the ancient myth
nor the old story re-told
but this:

> *from all our troubles*
> *we have been set free*

tears fell
beyond the blue
stained glass marbles,
those penetrating eyes
searing down in love
from the mahogany
rafters, where the
silver-haired man
stood polishing the pews.

This is what we ask for.

To ingest the living freedom

here in the hymn of solitude.

See, *is there anything too difficult?*

Let the rhetorical question

float in the room a moment.

Then, the immanent Logos answers.

Cryptography of Soul

Sit still.
Allow the thoughts to settle.
Breathe in.
Pause. Hold.
Exhale.
This is the isomer prescription.

And so you practice
wanting to arrive
at that heliocentric love.
They told you it was there.

Nothing.
Nothing.
Years of nothing.

You theorize that
you're doing it all wrong, and the
priest says, "get rid of sin"
the minister says, "recite Bible verses"
the guru says, "don't cling to experience"
and you, dutifully, do
all of these.

Still nothing.

But then, in a moment
of transparent awareness,
some might even call it
enlightenment,
a recollection:

> the urge to help the elder with her bags in the snow
> giving the little girl a Ritz cracker when she was crying
> serving eight lonely people Christmas dinner
> *and so on. . .*

Memories of unnoticed compassion moments
enter like swans
flying overhead against a
blue afternoon sky,
forming the karyotype
of allelic faith frequencies
never taught in that sermon.
Sit still.
Allow the thoughts to settle.
Breathe in. Pause. Hold.
Exhale. . .

Alternation of Generations

It's winter again.

The icicles hang off
the roof edge like
strung daggers,
thick snow-packed slabs slick
walkways and roadways
urging vigilant caution.

Then, there were the years of caution

and praying. The untying of
knots and prayers to the
holy family for the one
blessed gift that sustained
humankind through epochs
of cave dwelling and igloos,
family parlor gatherings with
cocktails, singing Christmas hymns
around the piano, and back yard barbeques.

But this selected phenotype, a family of three,
loving and living together,
connected, communicating,
presents a new three-dimensional configuration,
letting the old, structured paradigm go,
and with it, maybe, the discovery of
a little hope.

Or, a lot.

Comfort comes now
in forms remembered,
external in a centripetal hug,
internal in megaton gratitude.
The train whistle blows at 5am,
a friend shows up with a truck full of wood.

Solstice Morning Firstlight

In the cloistered quiet
of a dark winter morning,
it feels as if the world is asleep.
The noble expanse of sky
is just waking, again,
clothed in a nightgown
flowing in veiled layers of soft color.
In a chemotaxis of soul, the gradient
of sky attracts me straight into the embrace of God.
The neighbor's kitchen light is on.
Ever-moving pink-lipped clouds
kiss their way across the holy crepuscular sky.
The world is an altar.
I rise,
light a candle,
and pray.

Biome

This morning,
calm peacefully rests
over the naturescape of sky and tree
out my early meditation window,
draping even the air in
tranquil harmony.
The bare silhouette of
a mighty tree branch mimics
a sculpture of stillness against
a pale lavender and blue awakening sky.
Silence holds the sound, a creek
in the wall, the radiator hiss;
all speaking together as one
voice of resolute communion,
to find the space between
the fright still stuck in my heart
and the pull of proven trust.

And I wonder: how can these hidden pests
exist with *this* out my window?

Ancient Commensalism

It was an unlikely kind of day to be out in the garden.
Patches of snow still lingering in places,
slowly melting at the crusted edges
by the cool, softly falling rain. Oh, I know,
I don't usually like to walk in the rain,
especially on the precipice between
winter's departure and spring's
early, slushy entrance.
But after this long interval
of indoor contemplation, I just had
to reconnect with rain and mist,
frozen mud and the scent of the
moss once again. It feels new to me every year—
why am I still surprised even after
decades of the birthed vernal beginnings?
Today the real quest was to see
if the moss survived the winter,
so, I rounded the corner, through the
worn wooden fence door that creaked
a slow arthritic groan on opening. And there,
a vibrant minty green oasis in a landscape
of brown and ice, a MN winter desert.

I knelt down and touched the wet, cold cushioned tufts

in a posture of prayer.

I bowed close to the scent of green, the

fragrant awakening, this ancient remembrance of divinity,

a sacramental encounter,

a rain-soaked sabbath.

Vignettes of Biotic Change

i.

Cold, dark freeze of winter drips away
drop by drop in a sculpture
carved by Spring's warm fingers

ii.

Each new year
young seeds are released
when pinecone dies

iii.

God's light always affords an arrival
like a spring of inner buds, but when I shy
from deserving that loving, the warm light of truth
and untapped blossoms demure to emerge

The Final Eucharist

I didn't think
it would end
this way, parade
confetti soaked in
a chalice of blood,
sneaking out the back
door in the middle of
the night unnoticed,
as the accolades of years,
what one calls "a contribution,"
are spilled onto the dusty sidewalk
for the street sweep to brush
into a dustbin of deprecation

The dark place is really the
only home now, retreating
into the comfortability of
the expectation of terror
because the stakes are too high
to risk again
the expectation of joy

So, I eat the communion bread
of faith in solidarity with
other cave dwelling trogolofauna—
the flat-nosed fruit bat, the Canadian
grizzly, adapted to a
consoling life
in the shadows

Every time I doubt,
I leave you a little bit more

Another Surrender

Let me just listen to the sound of rain
complying the blunt injustices
I do to myself
towards surrender
without condition or restraint

Let me just listen to the sound of rain
releasing the nagging temptation
to yield inner energies
into the haggle over will

Let me just listen to the sound of rain
conceding my small knowledge of the truth
that has led to uproar and confusion

Let me just sit in the warm rain
with the skim of the soft mist on my cheek
reminding me that I am here
a floating raft on the current of God

59 Years Past Her Poem

Second Thessalonians 1:11

Sit in the light.

Let the gospel of intelligence that is *you,*
teach within those dark interior walls, as it does
and be embraced
with this present ontology

Pulling confusion into wonder
letting that long
desire see fulfillment's arrival,
and in an unexpected
surge, a surprising
inner uprising fills a void
never before filled

Can you live with this allowance,
and can you call it joy?
Don't hold anything
back. It's over now.
The rescue ship
has come to the

shore of this desert

island. *It's real.*

Run into the open arms

of freedom; birth into fruition

your every desire for goodness.

Yes, it can be this way.

Of Cats and Clouds

I have been handed a language
that is supposed to join me to the infinite,
repeated syllables
that were, perhaps, to someone,
at some time, made of spun gold
but now have turned dishwater gray
with a thin film of weak bubbles around the rim

I was told— yes— I was taught
that this exclusively sacred language
encompassed all of the divinity,
it was to become my mother tongue,
and no other.
And in my smallness,
I believed the infinite
was contained in
prefabricated phrases, that were like a
doll house with tiny couches
and little fake sinks with pretend faucets
that of course didn't work,
in prayers like worn out shoes
and worth as much,
the same droning songs on repeat

But then. . . one morning
I woke up to a grey
heart-shaped cloud
framed by my morning window,
a wall hanging in the sky
set above a glowing sunrise altar

There was the dismal, stagnant,
heart cloud
ingesting, moment by living moment,
the bolting, soul-saturated
sacramental music of
the sunrise itself.
Unable to contain it any longer,
the heart cloud broke open into a wordless prayer
a rainbow burst right through it in color and light

The cat crawled close
bridging safety and
comfort in my lap
as we witnessed a transfiguration
of the sad little grey heart cloud
into a blooming roseate coral tinted magnificence
that mimicked a newly frosted cookie.
Then, as the ancient of days blazed its entrance
ever upward, the heart cloud greedily

absorbed every one of the trillions of photons
singing their never-ending chorus
honoring the morning sky by turning
a holy sunflower yellow

In a Franciscan ecology, the eternal voice spoke,
"Why are you resisting this?"
I vowed in response to a heed a new language
one that toasts the entire world as a sacrament
revealing the presence of God

The cat and I were inducted
into another kind of observance that morning
as the fusion jazz of the Uncreated Light
took spontaneous wake
in the liturgy of a melodious purr....

Here is the real message of redemption:
The infinite cannot be contained

ONWARD

In the chaos that can sometimes be our lives, we search for places where we can hide and find safety, places to receive healing, comfort, and peace. Our hearts, searching for meaning, or answers, or a way forward, often lapse into silent and sometimes unconscious prayer. These prayers take on so many forms. Sometimes, we question if God even hears us. We ask for help and guidance, even miracles. We wait. But, what of a prayer, *"Oh God, you know where I live"*? It is really a prayer of faith. It says in its mere seven words a whole lifetime of information. It says, I have told you everything I need. It decries a very long time in waiting for the answer. It says, God, we have a history. And it says, *you know where I am*, right here waiting for you to break through the invisible bars. This book, *Five White Swans*, represents that very place. The poems speak to where we can go to find God's voice for the many questions of the heart.

Oftentimes these harbors of safety and peace are found in natural spaces where the creatures simply live to tell us of the mysteries they have found in the excellencies of God's beauty. This very mystery came to me on a winter day driving into the city with my daughter Sophie to look at houses. It was time to move beyond the home that once held us, but was keeping us trapped in years of grief, in an old life we no longer lived. As we drove past a large cornfield covered with snow, out of the corner of my eye I saw what looked like an enormous updrift of snow from the middle of the field. It was such a strange sight. Was it a gust of wind? Sophie and I looked quickly at the strange phenomenon as we drove past and saw that it was not an updrift of snow at all. It was five gorgeous white swans taking off in flight from the carpet of white snow layered on the field. I immediately knew that this striking sight, so perfectly coordinated with the moment we were driving by, held some spiritual message. I learned that the spiritual significance of swans from several ancient traditions was one of divine revelation, faith, and transformation. That day was indeed a transformation for me, signifying a move out of the home we lived in for fourteen years. I truly needed a revelation from God, and a whole lot of faith, for the transformation to a new way of living for our family. Why *five* swans? Typically swans mate for life. One of the swans in that flock had lost a mate. I saw my own loss in that image, living in a flock without my life partner. It was a comfort and an inspiration knowing that one of those swans was courageously taking off into flight to some new destination without a spouse alongside. I was doing that, too. How grateful I was for those five swans and the message from nature they brought to me that day.

By engaging with the poems in this collection, it is my hope that this poetic pilgrimage into the biology of the world and a theology of insight may be an offering for you to expand your own spiritual practices into a fresh revelation of God, as the words unfold in the poem, "Imaginative Prayer":

> Recover nature, where you are,
> like on the day when you prayed in the
> cathedral not made with hands.
> Summon images that urged you,
> pray the gospel of imagination.
> Be bold as you bewitch faith
> into becoming what it has never been.

Perhaps by learning the language of nature, you might discover that there is a world of wonder and beauty right outside your own back door. Through this liminal space, a fresh experience of God's love and presence opens. You may never look at moss the same way, you may find unexpected delight in the bees buzzing in the garden, or you may be brave enough to reach out and touch a cloud. Explore what transformational messages the *Love that Created* will reveal in your encounters with nature.

This hopeful ecotheology in poetic form is much needed in the current global climate crisis facing humanity and our shared earthly home. We and the earth are in it together. Can we use this wisdom to re-invigorate our primal love for nature, to see the natural world as far more than resources to be used and exploited? I believe so. Perhaps as a species we need to re-envision our dependence on the natural world, and its dependence on us, knowing that in this relational encounter we reflect divine love, as put forth in these lines from "Being In Essence"

The divine degree of
creation is the content of Self-revelation.
If the hyphae connecting
every tree, the pigment in the
hummingbird's iridescent feather, the atom and molecule,
gene regulation, and enzyme-substrate perfection
—all that was created—
communicates messages of the beauty
and enduring love of the Being-in-essence
       how then shall we love and protect this world?

I have hope in our species that we will continue to move toward creative and innovative ways to restore the beauty and value of our world. In this way, we recover our own birthright connection to nature for all it holds for us in a vibrant ecospirituality that replenishes us emotionally, and physically. I believe that as we fall in love again with the gorgeous earth that permits us life, in turn, *we will protect what we love.* We have learned that the scientific facts and warnings from ecologists, climatologists, marine biologists, and atmospheric scientists do scant little to move the human species to action. Rather, this crucial dialogue has become a battle ground, fueling division, conspiracy, denial, and apathy. So, we may ask… *what can we do?* Is there any hope, any solution?

One way forward toward global healing for us as broken humans, and for the more-than-human family of creatures, *and* for the geology of our earthly home, might be through reaching the core of the human heart. If the scientific evidence can't reach us to reverse the destructive course we are on, perhaps the arts and spirituality can. The poems in this book are meant to do just that. This poetic pilgrimage toward an ecotheology and an eco-spirituality reveals that spirit is far more than religion, and that nature holds the gentle power to lead us into the happiness and fulfillment we are missing. Once we realize that we must come together, across all political, racial, socioeconomic, religious, cultural and gender divides, being of one mind, to be commit-ted to implementing the right technologies toward sustainable living and thriving for all, we may just find what we have been missing for so long. Our ultimate happiness comes from our con-nection to one another, to the earth, and to our spiritual center. This biocentric way of life is what allowed our hominin ancestors to become the successful species we are today, and it is time we return to our roots.

In this mystical ecospirituality, I pray that you may find life, abundant peace, and the Spirit's guidance, leading you onward to new dimensions of the rich spirituality that nature has offered all along.

Peace

-LW

Bibliography and Recommended Reading

Anderson, Wallace and David H. Watters, eds. *The Works of Jonathan Edwards Vol. 11, Typological Writings*. New Haven: Yale University Press, 1993.

Berleant, Arnold. "The Human Touch and the Beauty of Nature." In *Living in the Landscape: Toward an Aesthetics of Environment*, 59–84. Lawrence: University Press of Kansas, 1997.

Brumm, Adam, et al. "Oldest Cave Art Found in Sulawesi." *Science Advances* 13 (2021) 1–12. https://www.science.org/doi/10.1126/sciadv.abd4648

Brunner, Emil. *Revelation and Reason*. Translated by Olive Wyon. Philadelphia:PA: Westminster, 1946.

Chiotti, Roberto. "The Architecture of Eco-Theology: Towards a New Typology for Christian Sacred Space." *Religions* 13 (2002) 1–24. https://www.mdpi.com/2077–1444/13/1/29

Daigle, Gary, et al. "Canticle of the Turing." https://www.songlyrics.com/gary-daigle-rory-cooney-theresa-donohoo/canticle-of-the-turning-lyrics/

De Smedt, Johan, and Helen De Cruz. "Delighting in Natural Beauty: Joint Attention and the Phenomenology of Nature Aesthetics." *European Journal for Philosophy of Religion* 5.4 (2013) 167–186.

Eliade, Mircea. *The Sacred and the Profane*. New York: Harper & Row, 1961.

Hofmann, Dirk et al. "U-Th Dating of Carbonate Crusts Reveals Neandertal Origin of Iberian Cave Art." *Science* 359.6378 (2018) 912–915. https://www.science.org/doi/10.1126/science.aap7778

Hopkins, Gerard Manley. "The Caged Skylark." https://poemanalysis.com/gerard-manley-hopkins/the-caged-skylark/

Jonsson, Fredrik Albritton. "The Industrial Revolution in the Anthropocene." *The Journal of Modern History* 84 (2012) 1–17.

Kolbert, Elizabeth. *The Sixth Extinction*: An Unnatural History. New York: Picador, 2014.

Kipling, Rudyard. "The Glory of the Garden." *Poem Analysis*. https://poemanalysis.com/rudyard-kipling/the-glory-of-the-garden/

Lee, Sang Hyun, ed. *The Works of Jonathan Edwards Volume 21, Writings on the Trinity, Grace, and Faith*. Yale University Press, New Haven, 2003.

Livingston, James. *Anatomy of the Sacred*. Upper Saddle River: Pearson Prentice Hall, 2009.

Machado, Antonio. "Last Night While I was Sleeping." In *Border of Dream: Selected Poems*, 87. Port Townsend: Copper Canyon, 2004.

Mandoki, Katya. "Bio-aesthetics: The Evolution of Sensibility through Nature." *Contemporary Aesthetics* 15 (2017) 1–11.

McFarland, I. *The Cambridge Dictionary of Theology*. Cambridge: Cambridge University Press, 2011.

Moe-Lobeda, Cynthia. "Love Incarnate: Hope and Moral-Spiritual Power for Climate Justice." In *Ecotheology: A Christian Conversation*, edited by Kiara Jorgenson and Alan Padgett, 41–48. Grand Rapids: Eerdmans, 2020.

Moltmann, Jürgen. 2019, *The Spirit of Hope: Theology for a World in Peril*, Louisville, KY: Westminster John Knox, 2019.

Oliver, Mary. "Li Po and the Moon." In *Evidence*, 28. Boston, MA: Beacon, 2009.

———. "How Would You Live Then?" In *Blue Iris: Poems and Essays*, 12. New York: Penguin Random House, 2006.

———. "When Death Comes." In *New and Selected Poems Volume I*, 10. Boston: Beacon, 1992.

Otto, Rudolf. *The Idea of the Holy: An Inquiry into the Non-Rational Factor in the Idea of the Divine and its Relation to the Rational*. Oxford: Oxford University Press, 1950.

Paeth, Scott. "You Make All Things New: Jonathan Edwards and a Christian Environmental Ethic." *International Journal of Public Theology* 5 (2011) 209–232.

Painter, Betsy. *A Christian's Guide to Planet Earth: Why It Matters and How to Care for It*. Grand Rapids: Zondervan, 2022.

Pals, Daniel. *Nine Theories of Religion*. Oxford: Oxford University Press, 2015.

Park, H. "Anthropological Perspective on Pandemic, Human Behavior, and Mental Health." *Asia-Pacific Psychiatry* 13.1 (2021) 1–9.

Prum, Richard. *The Evolution of Beauty*. New York: Anchor Books, 2017.

Ramsey, Paul, ed. *The Works of Jonathan Edwards Vol 8, Ethical Writings*. New Haven: Yale University Press, 1989.

Ritchie, Sarah Lane. "Dancing Around the Causal Joint: Challenging the Theological Turn in Divine Action Theories." *Zygon* 52.2 (2017) 361–79.

Roszak, Piotr. 2021, 'Sacramental View of Creation: Denis Edwards on God's Presence in Natural World." *HTS Teologiese Studies/ Theological Studies* 77.3 (2021) 1–6.

Ruether, Rosemary. *Gaia and God: Ecofeminist Theology of Earth Healing*. New York: Harper Collins, 1994.

Rumi, Jalāl al-Dīn Muhammad. *Rumi Day By Day*. Translated by Maryam Mafi. Charlottesville, VA: Hampton Roads, 2014.

Schafer, Thomas, ed. *The Works of Jonathan Edwards Vol. 13, The 'Miscellanies', a–500*. New Haven: Yale University Press, 1994.

Strachan, Owen and Douglas Allen Sweeney. *Jonathan Edwards on Beauty*. Chicago: Moody, 2010.

Volf, Miroslav. *Flourishing: Why We Need Religion in a Globalized World*. New Haven: Yale University Press, 2015.

Whitley, David. *Cave Paintings and the Human Spirit*. New York: Prometheus Books, 2009.

Winslow, Lisanne and Walter Schultz. "The Solubility of Salt: A Theistic Account." *Theology and Science* 16 (2018) 107–125.

Winslow, Lisanne. "A Biotheology of God's Divine Action in the Present Global Ecological Precipice." *HTS Teologiese Studies/ Theological Studies* 78.2 (2022) a7357.

———. "An Ecospirituality of Nature's Beauty: A Hopeful Conversation in the Current Climate Crisis." *HTS Teologiese Studies/Theological Studies* 79.2 (2023) 1–10.

———. *A Great and Remarkable Analogy: the Onto-Typology of Jonathan Edwards*. Göttingen: Vandenhoeck & Ruprecht, 2020a.

———. "A Living Spring Perpetually Springing: Jonathan Edwards' Natural Imagery, Onto-Types and the Rise of Ecotheology." *Jonathan Edwards Studies*, 13.1 (2023) 1–23.

———. *A Trinitarian Theology of Nature*. Eugene: Wipf & Stock Publishers, 2020b.

Index of Terms and Nature Images

INDEX OF TERMS AND NATURE IMAGES

Author Bio

Photo by
Sophia Winslow

REV. DR. LISANNE WINSLOW holds a PhD in Cell Biology from Rutgers University and a PhD in Systematic Theology from the University of Aberdeen, Scotland. Dr. Winslow is currently a Visiting Fellow at Yale Divinity School while on sabbatical from her faculty post at the University of Northwestern-St Paul where she has been on faculty for more than two decades. She is an ordained minister in the Congregational Church and has served as Senior Minister at the Mendota Heights United Church of Christ in MN. Through her life work as a marine biologist, theologian, poet, and pastor, Dr. Winslow has unsealed a fresh awareness of the *Love that Created* through the beauty and value of the natural world. She has accomplished this with her students, members of her congregation, and the wider community through teaching, environmental lectures, and her numerous presentations in science and theology. Her unique engagement with nature bridges the disciplines of biology, theology, and the arts as she regularly leads people in nature prayer walks, meditation practice outdoors, sacred writing in nature, photography in nature as spiritual practice, and nature sketching. She has engaged an international community of scholars and seekers for two decades, that included a Fulbright Fellowship to Japan in 2009. The collection of poems in *Five White Swans* represents her tenth book of poetry. For the 2023–24 academic year, Dr. Winslow will be spending her third academic sabbatical conducting ecotheology research and writing as a Visiting Fellow at Yale Divinity School, residing near the sea in East Haven, CT, while living out a theology of nature with her daughters.